One day, a beautiful little girl named Pari was sitting next to a window. She was feeling sad because it was a gloomy day, and it was raining outside.

She ran to her room to get her telescope so she could see the colours of the rainbow more closely. Through the telescope, she observed that there were seven colours in the rainbow: RED, ORANGE, YELLOW, GREEN, BLUE, INDIGO, and VIOLET.

Suddenly, she noticed a rainbow in the sky. Seeing the rainbow made Pari very happy, and she started dancing with joy.

To her surprise, Pari heard a noise and realized the rainbow was talking! The colours of the rainbow were complaining that no one hears their voices or understands their feelings.
Pari smiled and said, “I would be glad to hear what you want to say.”

Red spoke first

“I represent the feeling of love. People should love more.”

Orange chimed in: “I bring the feeling of joy. People should be more joyful in life.”

Yellow added:
"I symbolize brightness. People should always hope for a bright future."

Green shared:
"I stand for growth. People should continue to learn and grow in life."

Blue mentioned:

“I represent trust. People should trust themselves and each other more.”

Indigo stated:
"I stand for honesty. People should be honest and not lie to one another."

Violet concluded:
“I represent creativity. People should be more creative.”

Pari was happy to hear all the colours and promised that she would try to include all these feelings in her life. Hearing this, all the colours came together and became the rainbow of feelings.

Activities for Kids

1. Draw Your Own Rainbow of Feelings:

- Use crayons, markers, or colored pencils to draw a rainbow.
- Label each color with the feeling it represents.
- Think about how you can show these feelings in your daily life.

2. Rainbow Dance Party:

- Put on some music and dance like Pari when she saw the rainbow.
- Imagine each dance move is a different color of the rainbow. How does love (red) make you dance? How about joy (orange)?

3. Feelings Journal:

- Keep a journal and write or draw about how you felt each day.
- Use the rainbow colors to describe your feelings.

4. Trust Walk:

- Pair up with a friend or family member.
- One person closes their eyes while the other guides them around safely, helping to build trust (blue).

5. Creative Craft Time:

- **Use art supplies to create something new, like a picture or a sculpture.**
- **Let your creativity (violet) shine!**
  By practicing these activities, you can bring the rainbow of feelings into your own life, just like Pari.

Inayatt Wadhwa

About the Author

Inayatt Wadhwa is a cheerful and creative six-year-old from Pathways School Gurgaon. With a big imagination, she loves telling stories and drawing colourful pictures. "The Rainbow of Feelings" is her first book, inspired by her fascination with rainbows and the magical feelings they evoke. Inayatt's story about Pari and the talking rainbow illustrates how each colour represents a special emotion everyone can share.

Inayatt hopes her book makes everyone smile and helps kids understand their feelings better. She enjoys reading, dancing, playing with her friends, and coming up with new stories. Inspired by her dad, Inayatt dreams of writing many more books that bring joy, fun, and creativity into everyone's lives.